MICROSCOPIC
Scary Creatures

Written by
Ian Graham

Created and designed
by David Salariya

BOOK HOUSE

Author:

Ian Graham studied applied physics
at the City University, London. He then took a
postgraduate degree in journalism, specialising in
science and technology. Since becoming a freelance
author and journalist, he has written more than
one hundred children's non-fiction books.

Artists:

Carolyn Scrace
Janet Baker and Julian Baker
    (JB Illustrations)
John Francis

Series Creator:

David Salariya was born in Dundee,
Scotland. In 1989 he established The Salariya Book
Company. He has illustrated a wide range of books
and has created many new series for publishers in the
UK and overseas. He lives in Brighton with his wife,
illustrator Shirley Willis, and their son.

Editor: Jamie Pitman

Editorial Assistant:
Rob Walker

Picture Research:
Mark Bergin, Carolyn Franklin

Photo Credits:

t=top, b=bottom

fotolia: 5t, 6, 10, 12, 18, 22, 23, 26
iStockphoto: 5b, 7, 21, 24, 27, 29

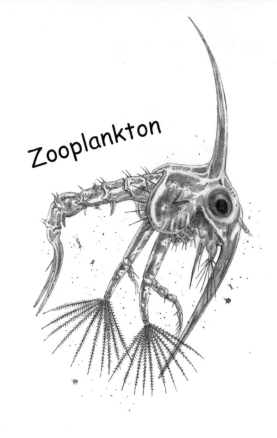

Zooplankton

Published in Great Britain in MMIX by
Book House, an imprint of
The Salariya Book Company Ltd
25 Marlborough Place, Brighton BN1 1UB

SALARIYA

A catalogue record for this book is available
from the British Library.

HB ISBN: 978-1-906714-07-9
PB ISBN: 978-1-906714-08-6

Printed in China

Visit our website at **www.book-house.co.uk**
or go to **www.salariya.com**
for *free* electronic versions of:
You Wouldn't Want to be an Egyptian Mummy!
You Wouldn't Want to be a Roman Gladiator!
Avoid Joining Shackleton's Polar Expedition!
Avoid Sailing on a 19th-Century Whaling Ship!

PAPER FROM
SUSTAINABLE
FORESTS

Contents

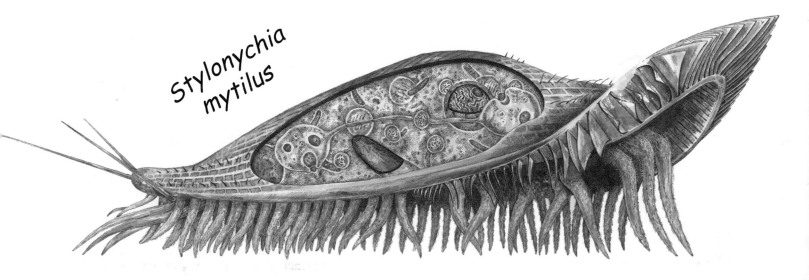

Stylonychia mytilus

What are microscopic creatures?

Cilia

Food particles move this way

Microscopic creatures are very small. Some of them are so small that they can be seen only with a powerful **microscope** such as an **electron microscope**. Others are just big enough to be seen with the naked eye, but you would need a microscope to see them clearly.

Although these creatures are tiny, some of them look like monsters from another world. The tiniest of these micro-monsters are called **protozoa**. They are made of just one living **cell**.

Stentor polymorphus (cutaway view)

Stentor polymorphus is a trumpet-shaped protozoan (single-celled animal) that lives in **fresh water**. It is just 1.2 mm long. It is covered with short hairs called **cilia**. The cilia around the trumpet's rim beat back and forth to sweep food particles down inside it.

Deer tick
(2 mm long)

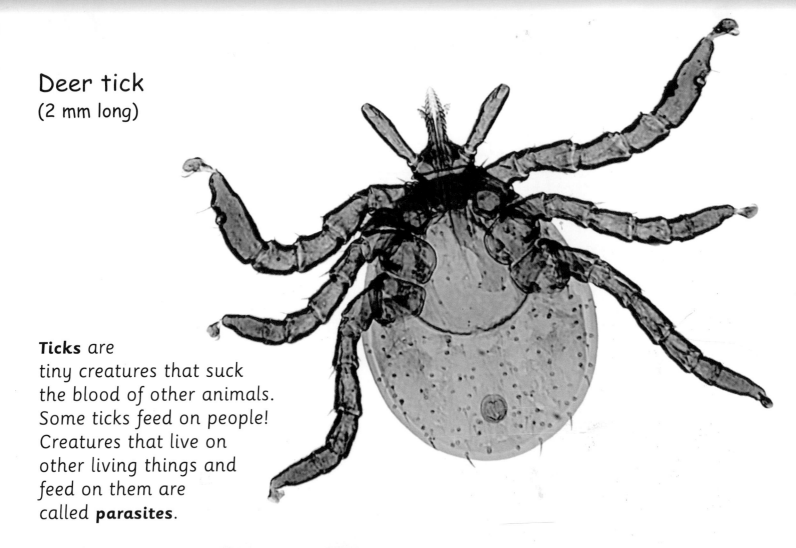

Ticks are
tiny creatures that suck
the blood of other animals.
Some ticks feed on people!
Creatures that live on
other living things and
feed on them are
called **parasites**.

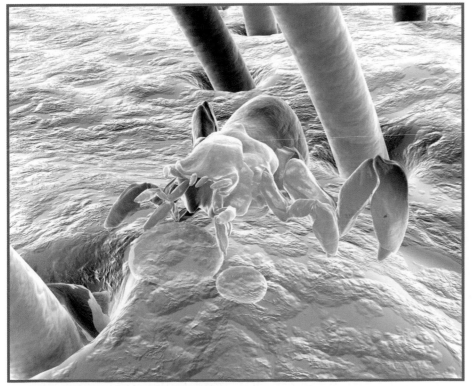

Mite seen through an electron microscope

Mites are tiny crawling
creatures less than a
millimetre long. Many of
them are a lot smaller.
They look like little black
dots, if you can see them
at all.

Mites and ticks have their
skeleton on the outside of
their body, like tiny crabs.
It's called an **exoskeleton**.
It protects the soft parts
of their body on the
inside. Having an
exoskeleton makes them
tough little creatures.

Where do micro-monsters live?

Microscopic creatures are found nearly everywhere. They live in rivers, the sea, soil, on garden plants and in forests. They live in soggy marshes and dust-dry deserts. They're found on top of mountains and at the icy poles. They even live in your home and on your body, but most are so small that you don't notice them.

Dust mites live in the dust and fluff in our homes.

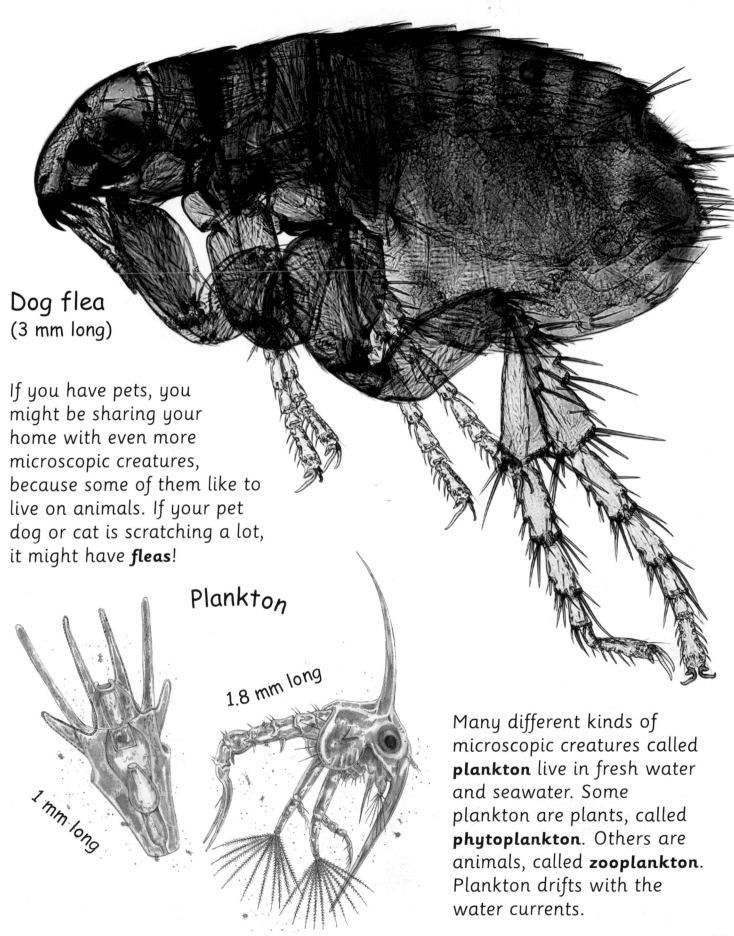

Dog flea
(3 mm long)

If you have pets, you might be sharing your home with even more microscopic creatures, because some of them like to live on animals. If your pet dog or cat is scratching a lot, it might have **fleas**!

Plankton

1.8 mm long

1 mm long

Many different kinds of microscopic creatures called **plankton** live in fresh water and seawater. Some plankton are plants, called **phytoplankton**. Others are animals, called **zooplankton**. Plankton drifts with the water currents.

How do such tiny creatures get around?

Most microscopic creatures move about so that they can hunt for food and escape from danger. Many of them get around by walking.

Fleas are great jumpers. They can suddenly leap high in the air to hop onto a passing animal or make a quick escape.

Some microscopic creatures that live in water can swim, but others don't move about at all. They stay in one spot and wait for food drifting in the water to come to them.

Rotifers are tiny creatures, measuring from 0.04 mm to 2 mm long, and made of about 1,000 cells. Their mouth is surrounded by cilia (hairs) leading down into their stomach. Some rotifers swim around. Others stay in one place, stuck to a rock.

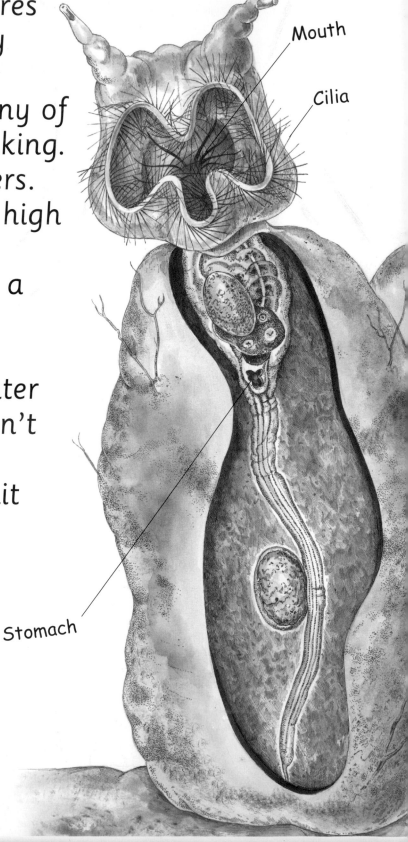

Rotifer
(cutaway view)

Mouth

Cilia

Stomach

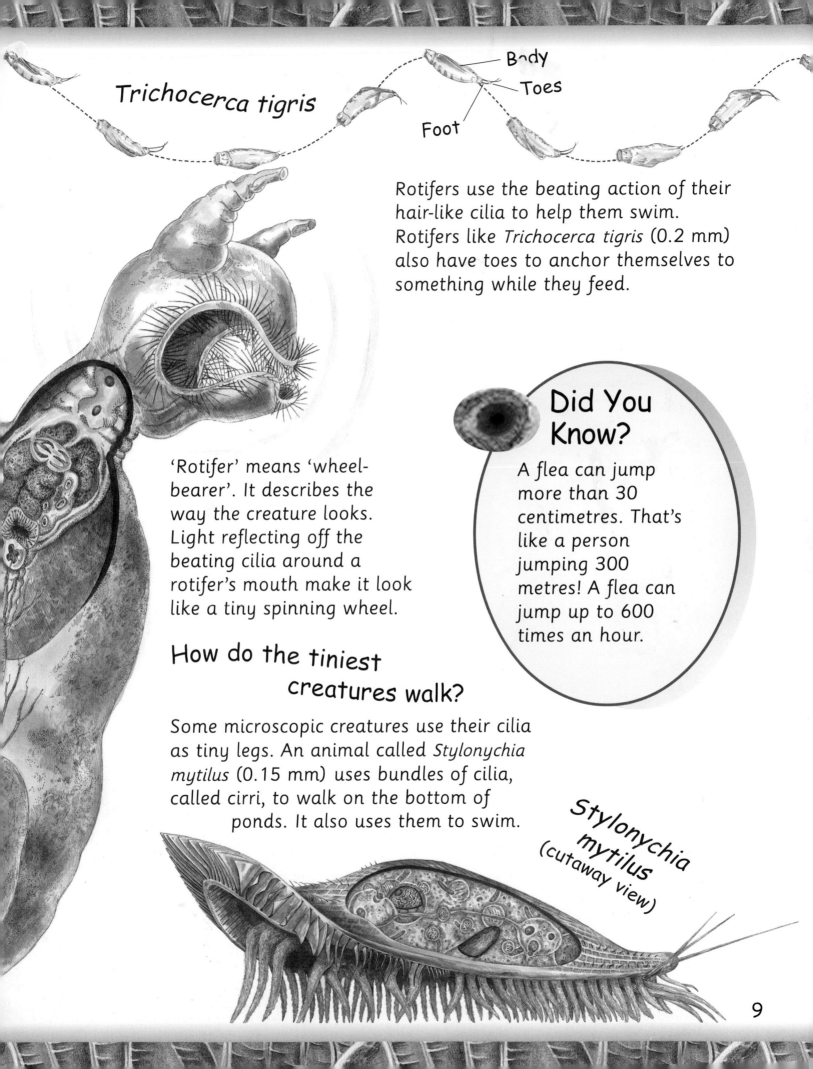

Trichocerca tigris

Body
Toes
Foot

Rotifers use the beating action of their hair-like cilia to help them swim. Rotifers like *Trichocerca tigris* (0.2 mm) also have toes to anchor themselves to something while they feed.

'Rotifer' means 'wheel-bearer'. It describes the way the creature looks. Light reflecting off the beating cilia around a rotifer's mouth make it look like a tiny spinning wheel.

How do the tiniest creatures walk?

Some microscopic creatures use their cilia as tiny legs. An animal called *Stylonychia mytilus* (0.15 mm) uses bundles of cilia, called cirri, to walk on the bottom of ponds. It also uses them to swim.

Did You Know?

A flea can jump more than 30 centimetres. That's like a person jumping 300 metres! A flea can jump up to 600 times an hour.

Stylonychia mytilus (cutaway view)

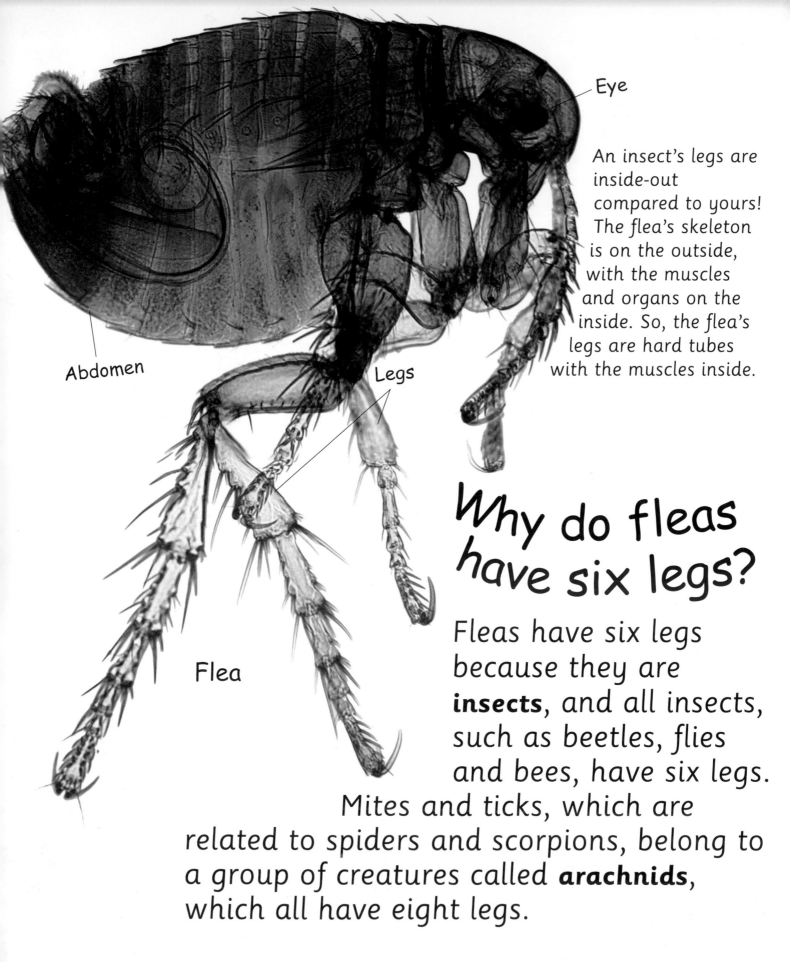

Eye

Abdomen

Legs

Flea

An insect's legs are inside-out compared to yours! The flea's skeleton is on the outside, with the muscles and organs on the inside. So, the flea's legs are hard tubes with the muscles inside.

Why do fleas have six legs?

Fleas have six legs because they are **insects**, and all insects, such as beetles, flies and bees, have six legs. Mites and ticks, which are related to spiders and scorpions, belong to a group of creatures called **arachnids**, which all have eight legs.

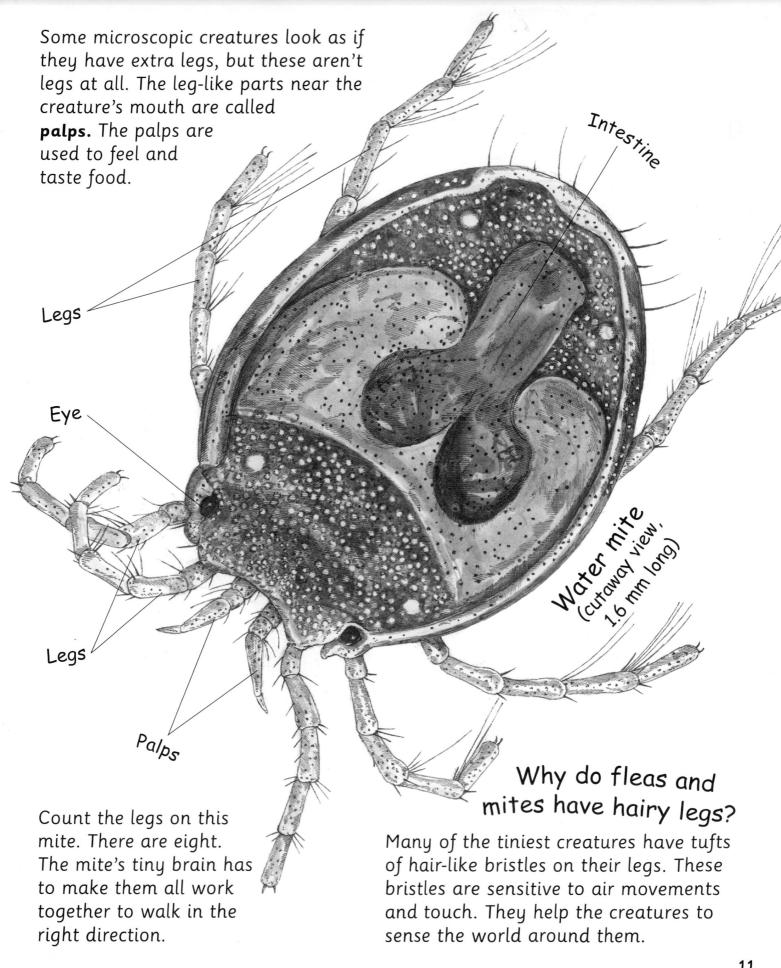

Some microscopic creatures look as if they have extra legs, but these aren't legs at all. The leg-like parts near the creature's mouth are called **palps.** The palps are used to feel and taste food.

Legs

Intestine

Eye

Legs

Palps

Water mite (cutaway view, 1.6 mm long)

Count the legs on this mite. There are eight. The mite's tiny brain has to make them all work together to walk in the right direction.

Why do fleas and mites have hairy legs?

Many of the tiniest creatures have tufts of hair-like bristles on their legs. These bristles are sensitive to air movements and touch. They help the creatures to sense the world around them.

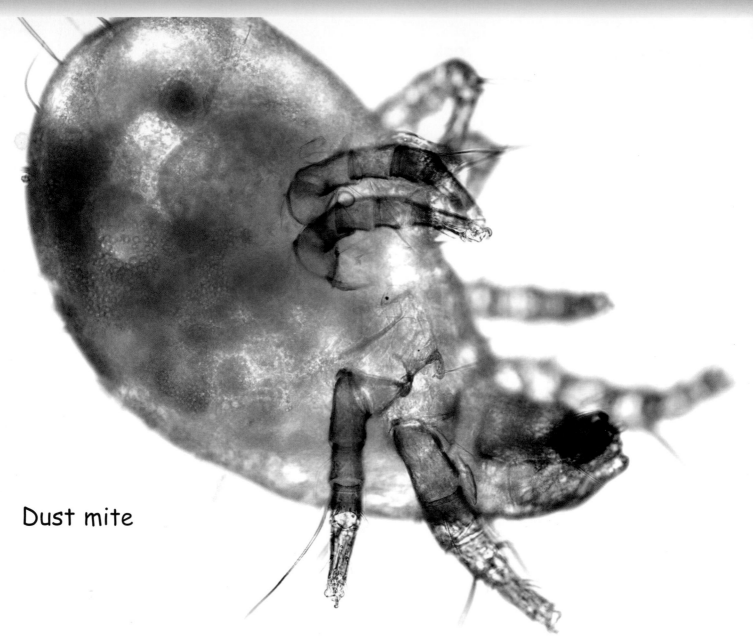

Dust mite

What do micro-creatures eat?

Tiny creatures eat tiny things. Dust mites eat flakes of skin which they find in the dust in your home. Lots of microscopic creatures feed on plants. Some have sharp jaws for munching through leaves, while others have needle-like mouth parts for making holes in plants to suck out sap.

What are predators?

Predators are creatures that hunt and kill other creatures for food. Some microscopic creatures are predators. *Actinosphaerium eichhornii* is a predator. It's just one big ball-shaped cell, 0.8 mm across, with lots of spiny arms sticking out. It drifts around freshwater ponds and lakes, sticking bits of food with its arms and digesting them.

Actinosphaerium eichhornii
(cutaway view)

How do blood-suckers feed?

Fleas and ticks have mouth parts that are strong and sharp enough to cut through an animal's skin. Then they suck out blood.

Did You Know?

In just one day, a cat flea can suck as much as 15 times its own body weight in blood out of a cat.

How long do they live?

Small creatures usually have shorter lives than large creatures, and the smallest creatures don't live long at all. Most microscopic creatures live for just a few weeks or months.

   Tiny parasites called head lice live for only about a month, but they can lay up to 300 eggs in this short time. Most fleas and dust mites live for only three months or so. Ticks, however, can live from several months to two years.

What are water bears?

Water bears are tiny creatures, about 1 mm long, that live in fresh water. If their bodies dry up, they can survive for many years and come back to life when water returns.

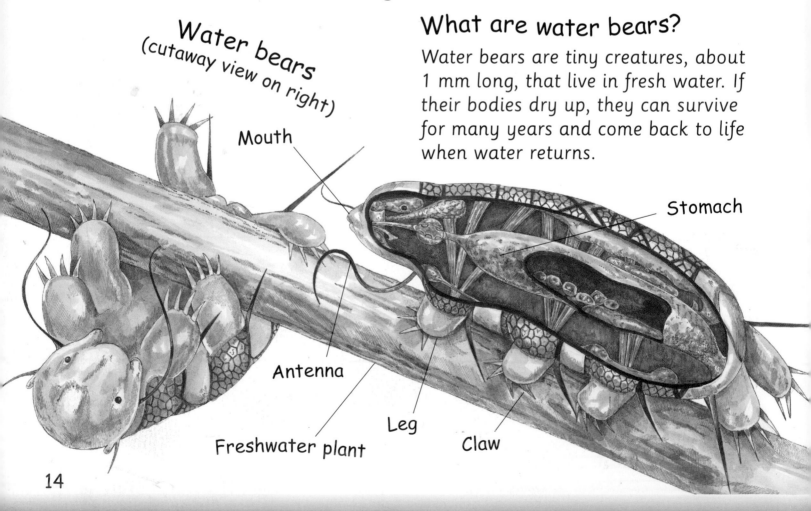

Water bears
(cutaway view on right)

Mouth

Stomach

Antenna

Leg

Freshwater plant

Claw

Did You Know?

When dried-up water bears were sent into space aboard a satellite, they returned unharmed, making them the first animals to survive in the **vacuum** of space.

How long does a water flea live?

The length of a water flea's life depends on the temperature of the water it lives in. At 20°C, it lives for 7 to 8 weeks. In colder water, its heart beats more slowly, and it lives longer.

How do cat fleas find cats?

An adult cat flea emerges from a **cocoon**. It can delay coming out of its cocoon for several months until a cat walks by. When the flea feels the warmth of a nearby cat or feels the vibration of its footsteps, it quickly comes out of the cocoon, leaps onto the cat and starts sucking its blood.

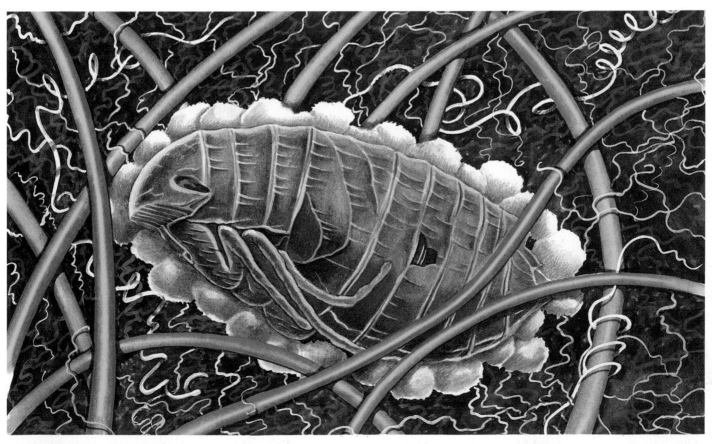

Cat flea in silk cocoon

Can such small creatures bite me?

Each kind of animal has its very own parasite, which could be a flea, a louse, a mite or another microscopic creature. The animal a parasite lives on is called the **host**. There are some kinds of fleas, lice and mites that only live on people, and many of them are biters. They bite you to eat your skin or drink your blood!

Cat fleas and dog fleas will bite people too, but they cannot produce eggs unless they bite cats or dogs. They have to feed on the right sort of blood.

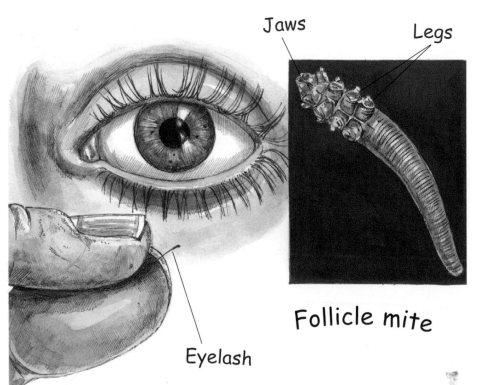

Jaws

Legs

Follicle mite

Eyelash

Long thin follicle mites (0.2–0.3 mm long) live inside hair follicles, the holes in the skin that hairs grow out of. They feed on skin cells and an oily substance called sebum that the follicle produces, so they don't have to bite. They live mainly on a person's face and head, especially in the eyelash follicles.

Mountain beaver

Beaver fur

Mountain beaver flea (enlarged)

Actual size

Did You Know?

There are more than 2,000 **species** of fleas. Cat fleas are found on both dogs and cats in North America. Dog fleas are more common in Europe.

Most fleas are 2–3 millimetres long. It's bad enough to be attacked by these tiny creatures, but spare a thought for the mountain beaver.

Mountain beavers live on the west coast of North America. They are host to the world's biggest flea. It's called *Hystrichopsylla schefferi* and it is 12 millimetres long, or four to six times the size of other fleas!

Why do such tiny bites itch so much?

The bites of fleas and ticks are no bigger than a pin-prick, but they can get very red, swollen and sore. It's not the bite itself that causes the itching and pain. It's the creature's saliva, or spit, that causes trouble. Scabies mites are microscopic creatures that burrow into human skin. They eat the skin as they dig through it, and their saliva causes terrible itching.

X-Ray Vision

Hold the next page up to the light and see what's under the skin.

See what's inside

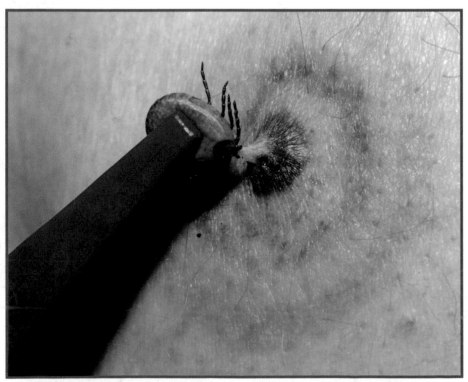

A tick being removed from human skin

Ticks are blood-sucking creatures that usually feed on pets and wild animals. However, they will bite humans too. A bite from a tick usually causes a mild itching, but some people can suffer a much more painful reaction.

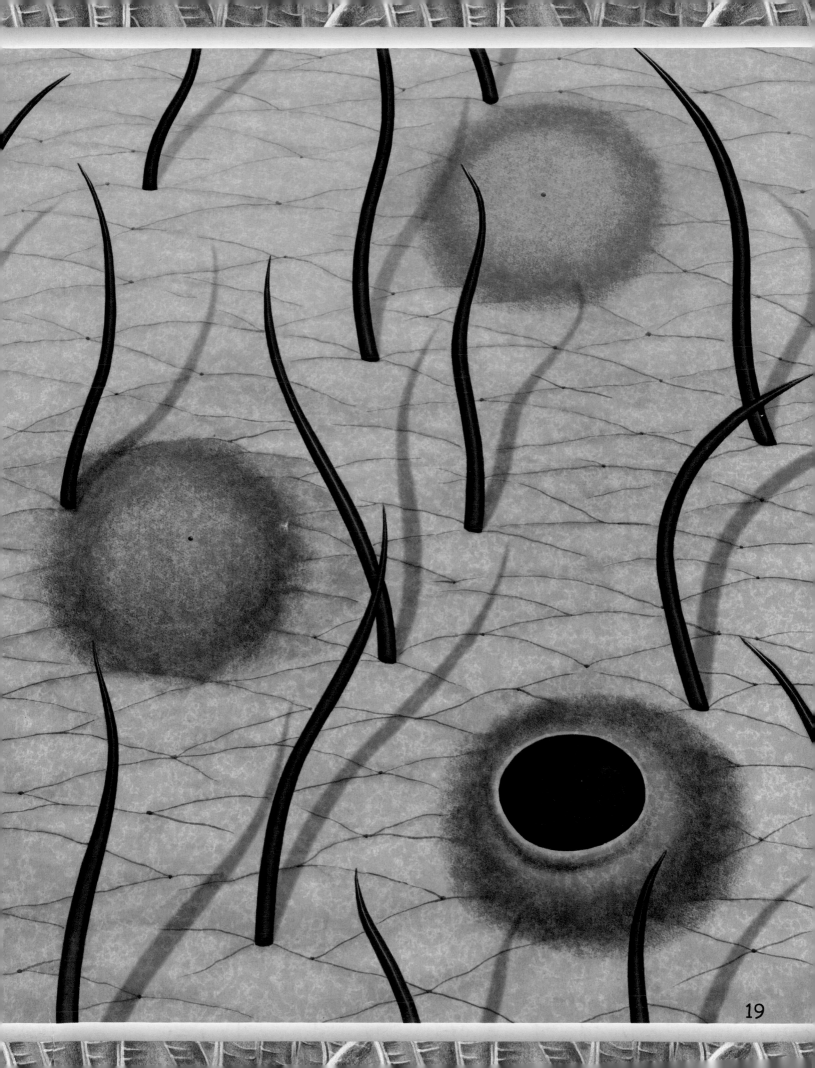

19

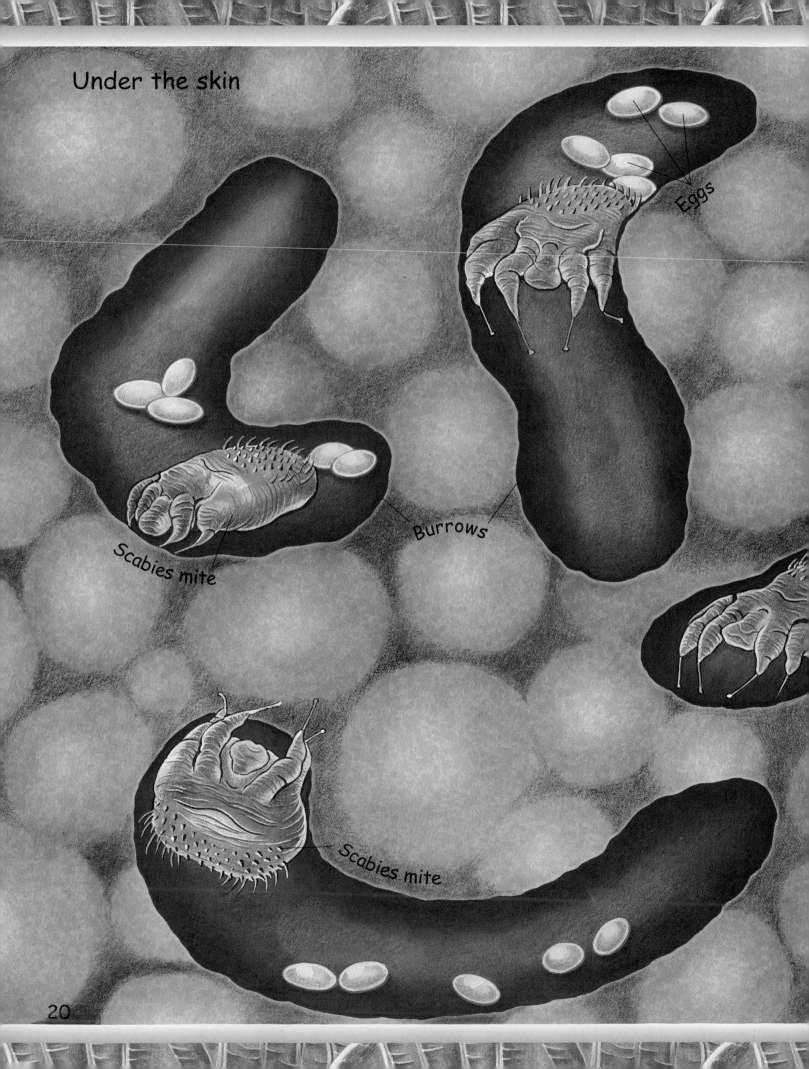

Under the skin

Eggs

Burrows

Scabies mite

Scabies mite

Are micro-monsters dangerous?

Some microscopic creatures are dangerous to people and animals because they cause diseases. A serious disease called malaria is caused by a tiny organism called plasmodium, which is spread by mosquito bites. Another serious disease called sleeping sickness is caused by parasites which are spread by bites from tsetse flies.

Did You Know?

Every year up to 500 million people around the world are infected with diseases spread by mosquito bites. Almost 3 million of them die.

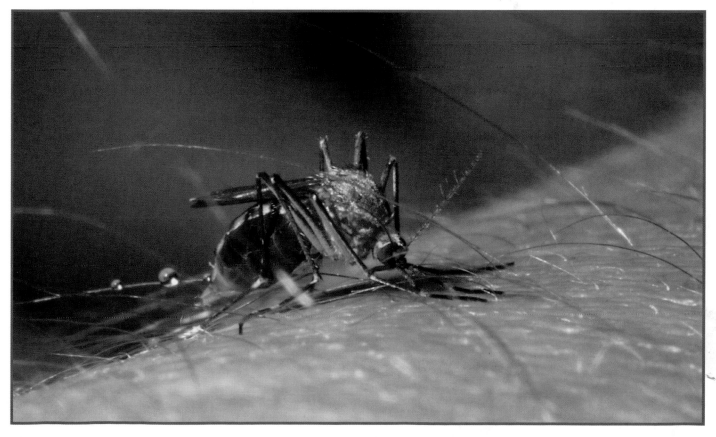

Mosquito piercing human skin and taking a meal of blood

How do biters find their victims?

Most microscopic creatures can't see, but they have other ways of finding food. They focus on the victim's body heat, its breath or the vibrations it causes when it moves.

Some microscopic creatures drift about in water, waiting for a victim to walk through it or drink it. Others are carried to their victims by infected flies and mosquitoes.

Young wood ticks cling to bushes, but quickly fasten themselves upon the bodies of any passing animal.

Human head louse
(seen through a microscope)

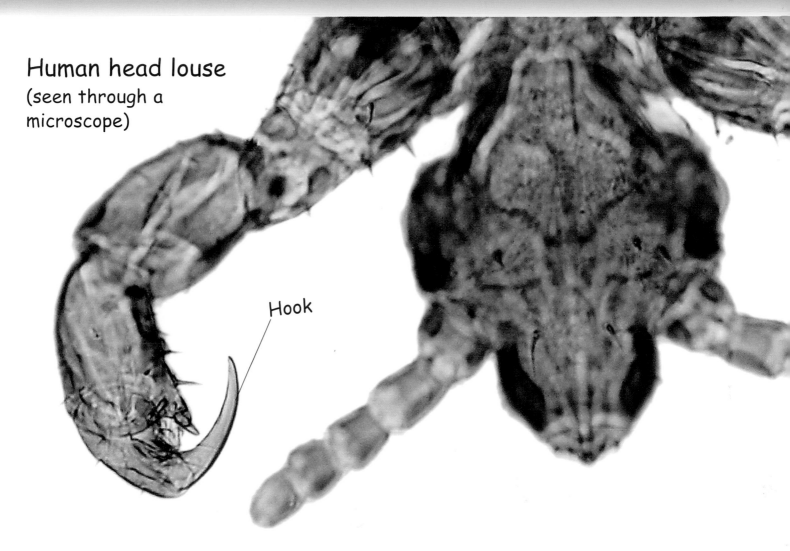

Hook

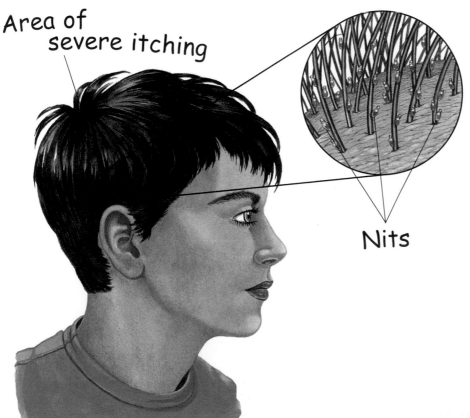

Area of severe itching

Nits

How do they hold on?

Creatures have developed special ways to hold on to their host when it moves or scratches to get rid of them. Head lice have hooked legs that grip hair tightly. When they lay eggs, they stick the eggs to strands of hair to stop them falling off. The eggs are called nits.

What do micro-monsters do to plants?

Microscopic creatures may be tiny, but they can damage and even destroy plants.

X-Ray Vision

Hold the next page up to the light and see what's eating the wheat.

See what's inside

Insects called thrips, less than a millimetre long, make holes in plants and suck out the sap. Holes made by thrips and other creatures also let in viruses, bacteria and fungi, which cause even more damage to the plant.

Spider mites are tiny arachnids that feed on plant sap. Thousands of mites can suck out so much sap that a plant's leaves turn yellow and die. Without enough leaves to make food, the plant may die as well.

Red spider mite from Kenya, Africa

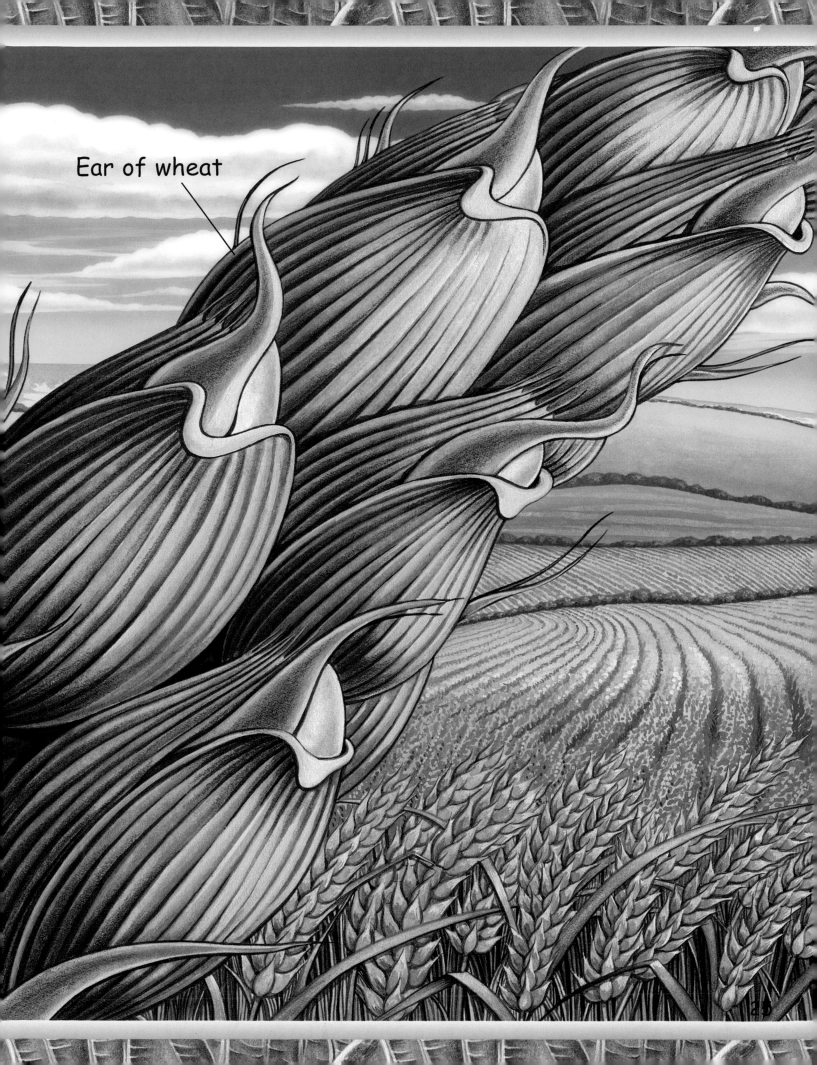

Ear of wheat

Thrips

26

What are larvae?

When the egg of a tiny insect such as a flea hatches, the wormlike creature that comes out is called a **larva**.
    The larva grows for a while and then seals itself inside a hard case or cocoon. Inside, it becomes a **pupa**, which then changes into the adult insect. Some sea creatures, such as shrimps, crabs and lobsters, start their lives as microscopic larvae too.

Did You Know?

When a cat flea larva spins a cocoon around itself, bits of fluff stick to the cocoon and make it look like a harmless bit of carpet fluff.

Breathing tube

Water's surface

Larva

Larva

Pupa

Mosquito larvae and pupa

Can microscopic creatures be good for us?

Not all microscopic creatures are nasty **pests** or a cause of disease. Some of them can be helpful. One way to deal with the pests that damage plants is to attack them with creatures such as tiny flies and wasps instead of chemicals. Using creatures in this way is called 'biological control'.

How can wasps help us?

A tiny wasp, called *Encarsia formosa* (only 0.6 mm long), is used to control a greenhouse pest called whitefly. The wasps lay their eggs inside the whitefly. When the eggs hatch, the grubs eat the whitefly alive!

How do cows use microscopic creatures?

Cows eat a lot of grass, which contains a substance called **cellulose**. Most animals can't digest cellulose, but the bacteria and protozoa in a cow's stomach digest the cellulose for it. One of the protozoa that do this vital job is called *Diplodinium ecaudatum*.

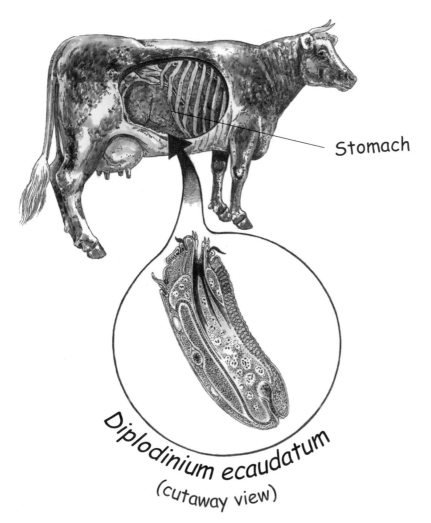

Stomach

Diplodinium ecaudatum
(cutaway view)

Did You Know?

Garden slugs can be controlled by microscopic worms called nematodes. The worms multiply inside the slugs and kill them from within.

This tomato hornworm, a pest, is covered with cocoons of wasps that hatched inside it and ate their way out.

Microscopic facts

Mites are among the oldest known creatures. There are fossils of mites as much as 400 million years old. There are more than 45,000 known species of mites, but scientists think there are a lot more still to be discovered.

The mattress on a bed can have up to 10 million dust mites living in it! Half a teaspoonful of dust can contain up to 500 dust mites.

An insect's pupa can't move. It can't run away from a predator, so larvae hide themselves away before they change into a pupa. Pupae are often coloured to match their surroundings, or disguised so they're hard to spot.

A flea's body is tall and thin. This makes it easy for the flea to squeeze through an animal's fur, hair or feathers.

If a flea were to lay eggs and the resulting fleas kept breeding, there would be 10,000 fleas in just one month!

On each of a tick's first two legs is a part called Haller's organ. It senses heat and carbon dioxide. Ticks feed on warm-blooded animals which breathe out carbon dioxide. Haller's organ helps ticks to find their victims by tracking the carbon dioxide.

After taking a meal of blood, some ticks need to move on to another host before they can continue to the next stage of their life cycle.

Plankton

Ticks can spread a variety of diseases to people, pets and wild animals. One of these is called Lyme disease. It causes joint and muscle pains and swollen glands. In some cases, it can be a very serious illness.

When your skin is cut and bleeds, the bleeding soon stops. The blood thickens and forms a clot that plugs the cut. This is called coagulation. When a flea or tick bites through the skin, it injects a substance called an anticoagulant. It stops the blood forming a clot, so the blood keeps flowing and the flea or tick can keep feeding.

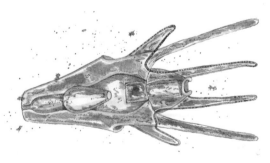

Glossary

arachnid An eight-legged animal. There are more than 50,000 different species of arachnid.

cell The smallest unit, or building block, of a plant or animal.

cellulose The substance that makes up most of a plant's cell walls.

cilia Tiny hair-like parts of a cell. Some cilia beat back and forth to guide food into a creature's mouth; others may help it to swim.

cocoon A protective case which houses an insect in its pupal stage.

exoskeleton A skeleton that covers the outside of a creature.

flea A wingless blood-sucking insect, a parasite that lives on warm-blooded animals.

fresh water Water from lakes and rivers which, unlike seawater, is not salty.

host The animal or plant that a parasite lives on.

insect A small animal with six legs and an exoskeleton.

larva (plural **larvae**) A wormlike creature that hatches from an insect egg. After a time, the larva changes into an adult creature.

microscope A scientific tool that uses lenses to produce magnified images of small objects. An **electron microscope** is especially powerful.

microscopic So small that it can only be seen through a microscope.

mite A tiny eight-legged creature related to spiders.

palps Feelers for touch or taste on the head of an insect or other small creature.

parasite A small creature that lives on a larger creature and feeds from it.

pest A plant or animal which is harmful, especially to humans.

plankton Small plants (**phytoplankton**) and animals (**zooplankton**) that drift with water currents in seas, rivers, lakes and ponds.

predator A creature that kills and eats other creatures.

protozoan (plural **protozoa**) An animal consisting of only one cell.

pupa The stage of an insect's life when it changes from a larva into an adult insect.

rotifer A tiny creature that lives in water, with circles of beating cilia at one end that look like spinning wheels.

species A group of animals that are so similar to each other that they can breed with each other.

tick A small eight-legged blood-sucking creature related to spiders.

vacuum A place with no air in it, such as outer space.

Index